I0815363

DiscoverRoo
An Imprint of Pop!
popbooksonline.com

The Eras of Taylor Swift

THE MIDNIGHTS era

Track List

1. Lavender Haze
2. Maroon
3. Anti-Hero
4. Snow on the Beach (ft. Lana Del Rey)
5. You're on Your Own, Kid
6. Midnight Rain
7. Question...?
8. Vigilante S—
9. Bejeweled
10. Labyrinth
11. Karma
12. Sweet Nothing
13. Mastermind

by Grace Hansen

WELCOME TO DiscoverRoo!

This book is filled with videos, puzzles, games, and more! Scan the QR codes* while you read, or visit the website below to make this book pop.

popbooksonline.com/Midnights

abdobooks.com

Published by Pop!, a division of ABDO, PO Box 398166, Minneapolis, Minnesota 55439.

Printed in the United States of America, North Mankato, Minnesota.

082025
012026

Cover Photo: Alexandra Tarasova (BigArtLab); Shutterstock Images

Interior Photos: Getty Images; Nathaniel Noir/Alamy Stock Photo; PaoloV/Flickr; Raj Valley/Alamy Stock Photo; Shutterstock Images; The Canadian Press/AP

Editors: Elizabeth Andrews and Anna Schwartz

Series Designer: Laura Graphenteen

Library of Congress Control Number: 2025940988

Publisher's Cataloging-in-Publication Data

Names: Hansen, Grace, author.

Title: The Midnights era / by Grace Hansen

Description: Minneapolis, Minnesota : Pop!, 2026 | Series: The eras of Taylor Swift | Includes online resources and index

Identifiers: ISBN 9781098248727 (lib. bdg.) | ISBN 9781098249243 (ebook)

Subjects: LCSH: Swift, Taylor, 1989- --Juvenile literature. | Popular music--Juvenile literature. | Popular (Songs, etc.)--Juvenile literature. | Albums--Juvenile literature. | Concerts--Juvenile literature. | Mass media and music--Juvenile literature.

Classification: DDC 782.42164097--dc23

*Scanning QR codes requires a web-enabled smart device with a QR code reader app and a camera.

TABLE OF CONTENTS

CHAPTER 1

BACK TO REALITY

After the dreamy and fictional albums *evermore* and *folklore*, Taylor was ready to get back to reality. She hit the **studios** in Brooklyn, Manhattan, and Los Angeles to record what she described as her "first directly **autobiographical** album in a while."

WATCH A VIDEO HERE!

Meet Taylor

Birthday: December 13, 1989
Star Sign: Sagittarius
Place of Birth: West Reading, PA
Favorite Number: 13
Favorite Color: Purple
Favorite Food: Chicken tenders and a chocolate shake

13

Benjamin Button

X O X O

Olivia Benson

Taylor Swift

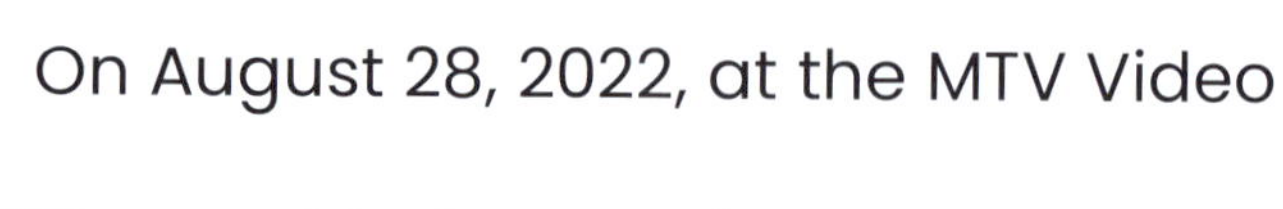

On August 28, 2022, at the MTV Video Music Awards, Taylor announced that she would be releasing her tenth studio album. Later that night, Taylor revealed the album art on her social media accounts.

Her Instagram post read, "*Midnights*, the stories of 13 sleepless nights scattered throughout my life, will be out October 21."

Taylor came bejeweled to the 2022 MTV Video Music Awards.

Taylor decided not to release any **singles**. When the album dropped on October 21 at midnight, people began to understand why. *Midnights* was meant to be enjoyed as a whole. Taking in the entire album in one sitting was the ultimate listening experience.

MIDNIGHTS 3AM EDITION

Three hours after Taylor released *Midnights*, she dropped the extended version of the album called *3am Edition.* The album featured seven additional tracks. The song "Would've, Could've, Should've" was praised by many people, who said it was the highlight of the extended album. Taylor wrote the song with musician Aaron Dessner.

CHAPTER 2

A PERFECT TEN

Midnights became the best-selling album of the year after just one day of sales. It received a 5-star review from *Rolling Stone*. And ten of the album's songs took the top 10 spots on both Apple Music and Spotify. It also made Taylor the first artist to win Album of the Year four times at the **Grammy Awards**.

COMPLETE AN ACTIVITY HERE!

Midnights

The Midnights album art was inspired by album covers from the 1960s and 1970s, when albums often had a white border with the track list displayed on the front.

Swift and Antonoff have produced 11 of Swift's albums together.

Taylor wrote 11 of *Midnights'* 13 tracks with longtime **collaborator** Jack Antonoff. The duo also **produced** the album together. Along with other artists, Swift and Antonoff brought together many different types of pop music to create the album's sound.

In the *Midnights* lyric booklet, Taylor asks fans, "What keeps you up at night?" Taylor later listed the themes of the album (and what keeps her up at night) clearly: "Self-loathing, fantasizing about revenge, wondering what might have been, falling in love, [and] falling apart."

Joe Alwyn and Taylor dated from 2016 to early 2023.

Secret Songwriter

The twelfth song on the album, "Sweet Nothing," was co-written by Taylor and William Bowery. William Bowery was the name Taylor's long-term boyfriend Joe Alwyn used when he wrote music with Taylor.

Though Taylor describes *Midnights* as a dark album, she also admits that she had fun making it. Each song is very self-reflective and shows how much she has grown as an artist and a person.

Midnights *had five different vinyl variations: Moonstone Blue, Jade Green, Blood Moon, Mahogany, and Lavender.*

Qualley and Alwyn filmed Stars at Noon *in Panama beginning in November 2021.*

Taylor also noted that *Midnights* might not have ever happened if it weren't for Joe Alwyn and Antonoff's then-fiancée, actress Margaret Qualley. Alwyn and Qualley filmed a movie together in Panama. The couples' time apart inspired the love songs on the album.

CHAPTER 3

BEHIND THE LYRICS

Taylor's 13 sleepless nights led to the 13 songs on *Midnights*. Taylor has admitted that her favorite song on the album, and one of her favorite songs that she has ever written, is "Anti-Hero." She called the song "very honest" and stated, "I don't think I've delved this far into

EXPLORE LINKS HERE!

Taylor accepts the Song of the Year Award for "Anti-Hero" at the 2023 iHeartRadio Music Awards.

my **insecurities** in this detail before."

The song is about understanding and admitting to personal flaws. Taylor sings, "It's me, hi, I'm the problem, it's me" to express this.

Easter Egg

When Taylor announced her twelfth album, *The Life of a Showgirl*, fans gathered all the Easter eggs from the "Anti-Hero" music video. One example is the anti-hero version of Taylor who wears a sparkly orange and green outfit, the colors associated with the album.

Taylor wears this dress in the final shot of the "Bejeweled" music video.

"Bejeweled" was Taylor's way of pumping herself up to get back to her pop era. After spending years in what she describes as a "**metaphorical** forest" writing *folklore* and *evermore*, she needed the confidence to return to writing pop music.

"Lavender Haze" is one of the love songs on the album. Taylor first heard the phrase "lavender haze" in an episode of the television show *Mad Men*. She learned it was commonly used in the 1950s to describe the feeling of being in love. She said, "I thought it was really beautiful. And ... when you're in the lavender haze, you'll do anything to stay there."

Taylor seemed to have a lavender glow during her Midnights act of the Eras Tour.

Fans pose in front of a mural in London dedicated to Midnights.

"Karma" was written from a very happy place. It is Taylor's way of showing that she is proud of what she has survived and accomplished. While people who have wronged her are getting their bad karma, Taylor's karma is everything that is good in her life.

DID YOU KNOW?

Fans made friendship bracelets to exchange at the Eras Tour in honor of the song "You're on Your Own, Kid."

Swift and Antonoff (right) *celebrate* Midnights *winning Best Pop Vocal Album of the Year at the 66th Annual Grammy Awards.*

Taylor knew that "Mastermind" would take the 13th spot on the album. She said, "I put it last on the album, because I'm really proud of it." The song celebrates everything Taylor has done, from romantic relationships to her career, and being a woman in the spotlight. She plays on the idea that she has planned and plotted every move.

Taylor announced her new album, The Tortured Poets Department, *during her Grammys acceptance speech.*

CHAPTER 4

GOOD KARMA

In an October 2022 interview, Taylor noted that it had been four years since she had toured. Years prior, Taylor was meant to take *Lover* on the road. However, the COVID-19 **pandemic** put an end to that plan. Taylor said she "missed the connection" that touring brought her and her fans. On November 1, Taylor announced the Eras Tour.

LEARN MORE HERE!

Taylor was spotted out and about in New York in November of 2021.

Fans combined eras in their tour looks.

The Eras Tour would be the first time fans would see *Lover*, *evermore*, *folklore*, and *Midnights* performed in concert. But they would also get to celebrate Taylor's career from its beginning and every era that brought her to this point.

Fittingly, Taylor closed out the concert with the *Midnights* Era. And she dedicated a whopping seven songs to the act: "Lavender Haze," "Anti-Hero," "Midnight Rain," "Vigilante S—," "Bejeweled," "Mastermind," and finally, "**Karma**."

Taylor changed the "Karma" lyrics at some shows to "Karma is the guy on the Chiefs" to reference her boyfriend Travis Kelce.

Deciding what song to end a concert on, especially one as epic as the Eras Tour, is an important decision. "Karma" was the perfect way to close out the show. It is a celebratory song. It also embraces the difficulties that come with

Taylor, her dancers, and her backup singers take a bow to close out the Eras Tour show!

years of hard work. The lyrics "Ask me what I learned from all those years / Ask me what I earned from all those tears / Ask me why so many fade, but I'm still here" brought concertgoers back to everything Taylor had experienced.

Throughout the creation of ten amazing **studio** albums, Taylor had survived broken relationships, people turning their backs on her, and years of unwanted media attention. Taylor's karma was being able to look out over thousands of loving fans each night.

Paper confetti rained down to end the show. The colors represented each of Taylor's albums. Fans later learned that the mysterious, orange-colored confetti was an Easter egg for The Life of a Showgirl.

MAKING CONNECTIONS

TEXT-TO-SELF

What is your favorite song from the *Midnights* Era? Why is it your favorite?

TEXT-TO-TEXT

Have you read books about any other music artists? How are they similar to or different from Taylor Swift?

TEXT-TO-WORLD

As a reader, why do you think so many people around the world connect with Taylor Swift and her music? Write a few sentences to explain your answer.

GLOSSARY

autobiographical — relating to a person's own life and experience.

collaborator — a person who collaborates. To collaborate is to work with someone else on a project.

Grammy Awards — an event that recognizes and awards remarkable works in music throughout the year.

insecurity — a lack of confidence in oneself.

karma — the belief that one's actions determine one's future in life.

metaphorical — referring to a figure of speech in which a word or phrase is used in place of another to suggest a similarity in meaning between them.

pandemic — an outbreak of a disease that spreads across the world.

produce — to organize the creation of music recordings.

single — a song that is released as a stand-alone from the album.

studio — a place where recordings are made.

INDEX

DiscoverRoo!
ONLINE RESOURCES

This book is filled with videos, puzzles, games, and more! Scan the QR codes* while you read, or visit the website below to make this book pop.

popbooksonline.com/Midnights

*Scanning QR codes requires a web-enabled smart device with a QR code reader app and a camera.